Do You Treat Your Pet As If It Were Your Child?

Other books by Barry Sinrod

The First Really Important Survey of American Habits
(with Mel Poretz)

The Baby Name Personality Survey
(with Bruce Lansky)

Do You Do It with the Lights On?
(With Mel Poretz)

Do You Do It When Your Pets Are in the Room?

Just Married
(with Marlo Grey)

The Baby Name Survey
(with Bruce Lansky)

The Do You Series

Do You Treat Your Pet As If It Were Your Child?
(with Marlo Mittler)

Do You Treat Your Pet As If It Were Your Child?

Barry Sinrod
and
Marlo Mittler

SelectBooks, Inc.
New York

First Edition

ISBN 1-59079-014-6

Library of Congress Cataloging-in-Publication Data
Sinrod, Barry and Mittler, Marlo
Do You Treat Your Pet As If It Were Your Child?-1st ed.

Manufactured in the United States of America

10 9 8 7 6 5 4 3 2 1

Dedication and Acknowledgements
(Barry)

I dedicate this book to all the pet lovers in the world. You are certainly among a group of people who truly go out of your way to provide special love to your pet. This is the second in what we hope is a never ending series of books under the umbrella title *Do You?* I want to thank Kenzi Sugihara of Select Books for helping to develop the idea and for his faith in all of the work that I have done previously. Without him there would be no *Do You* series.

If you have a pet, you will love this inside look at what makes a pet owner tick. You are a special "breed" (no pun) of person and you certainly do some really strange, interesting and funny things. Read the book and compare yourself to other Americans who have the love of a pet in common with you.

Of course, I give my extra special thank you to my lifelong love, my bride of nearly 40 years as we read this book and think of our own pets going back to the 1950s. To Grumpy (her "mutt" of a wonderful dog before we were married), to Freckles our wonderful beagle who was our "first child" before we started a family, then to one our greatest joys, Danny, our Old English Sheepdog. The tradition continues in our family as we now have three "granddogs" in addition to our six grandchildren. Lola and Luke belong to our son Blake and his wife Felice, and Sampson, a very, very large Newfoundland, is part of our daughter Jodey's family which includes husband David and grandchildren Alex, Cole and Jessie.

Barry

Dedication and Acknowledgements
(Marlo)

I dedicate this book firstly to my pets from my wonderful childhood. Danny (Old English Sheepdog), Ralph (Great Dane), Ollie (our cat), Benny (another cat), Sammy and Murray (our fish) and Sammy II (another fish). I don't think I realized how many other people loved their pets as much as our family did, until now!!

To my husband: Jordan. Just because I wrote about pets doesn't mean I am ready for us to get one! I know how much you want one just like your Golden Retreiver (Nugget) that you had as a kid. Right now, I think our three wonderful beautiful,special and perfect kids are enough. Ask me about a dog in a few years when we get past the diapers, sippy cups, and bottles galore, then I am sure I will be ready! The kids are already asking us "When can we get a puppy" everyday.

To Jodey, David, Alex, Cole and Jessie along with Blake and Felice. Thanks for allowing us to enjoy our "nephew-dogs" Samson (Newfoundland) and Luke (a good mix) and our "niece-dog" Lola (another mix) with their licks, leaps, drool, tail wagging, paws and all...until we get our very own...they sure are loveable!

Dad, thanks for the opportunity to continue writing with you, it is a sheer joy. Thanks to you and Mom for all you do, always! I love you!

Marlo

Introduction

When my daughter (Marlo) and I spoke to and met with several publishers, we met Kenzi Sugihara who took a look at all of our previous works and came up with the idea for a series of *Do You* books, we knew this is where we wanted to be.

In starting the *Do You* series we decided to revisit and update some of the subjects we have written about before. We added new questions and went back and asked some of the same questions again (some as far back as 15 years ago) to get the most up-to-date answers.

This book came about as a result of our family's love of all of our pets through the years.

This book is chock full of statistics that reveal the insides of the pet owning public of America. You will laugh, cry, be amazed and say, "that's just what we do." We would welcome any comments on anything in this book as well as ideas for new books. Simply go to our Website at **www.allaboutdoyou.com** and tell us what you think.

The Facts

The 21st century...It is still hard to believe that we are in a new century. Every day that passes brings new technology to our every day life. This entire book was written via the internet, finding the pet owners, interviewing them, getting the questionnaires back, tabulating the results and writing it and even printing it.

We never ever asked for anyone's name. The questions as you will see are sometimes private, everything goes, no holds barred! Having been a marketing researcher for nearly 40 years, I know it is imperative that we give complete privacy to each and every respondent. The individual respondent names are never ever an issue, only the answers to the questions which appear in the book. Certain demographics are asked so that we can classify people by age, income, geography, etc.

All of this adds up to a fun time for all! We are confident that these people told us the truth, because as mentioned no names are attached anywhere. The statistical margin of error is plus or minus 3 percent.

Are you ready to see where you stand or should stand or might stand among your group of pet lovers?

Our fans have told us over the years that what they think they like most about our books is that they are great gifts and coffee table, bathroom and conversation pieces that bring out the best and sometimes worst of someone as they discuss what is inside this book.

We are flattered that many of the fine universities across this country have used our books in their psychology classes. We also want to thank MTV, *Saturday Night Live* and all the networks and *USA TODAY* for telling people about our books.

So sit back and relax and have a great time and be sure to share it with someone you love!

This section is devoted to the animal lovers who were kind enough to tell us the intimate details about themselves and their relationship with the pets they so dearly love.

We know that these stories will be similar to yours, they will also bring a smile and perhaps a tear to you but we are confident you will enjoy each and everyone of them.

They cover every possible subject that we have shown you in the book. So sit back, have your pet at your side and read these gems to him/her.

Note: All of these stories are true. They were submitted to us as part of our questionnaire. We have added the subtitles for your enjoyment.

When a man loves a woman!

He meets her and falls madly in love with her, she feels the same way. It is an extremely loving relationship, but... he is extremely allergic to her cat. So much so, that it is painful for him to enter her apartment and sometimes even her clothing causes him to have extreme allergic reactions. She loves him so much that she tells him that she will give the cat away to another family. Although she has had the cat for 3 years, she loves him so much that she would be willing to part with her wonderful pet. He feels so bad about the situation that he won't let her do that because she loves the cat so very much. He tells her to wait a while and he will see what he can do. After visits to several allergists he begins a series of painful and uncomfortable injections to try to rid him of the allergy. After six weeks he is completely cured from any reaction and now three's company and they were married two months ago.

If my husband knew about this he would kill me!

My husband is not all that fond of the six cats that we have. He always says, "why isn't one enough?" But I know he is just being a grouchy old man. I see him petting and rubbing and kissing all the cats when he thinks I am not looking. Well, several weeks ago I put a roast into the oven. Sat down in front of the TV with my little babies and four hours later, two of my babies were clawing away at my dress and my face. I had fallen asleep and I opened my eyes, only to discover the kitchen was filled with smoke. The roast should have only been in the oven for two hours, not four. My kitties saved my life. If either the house had burned down or if there was any damage, my husband would have killed me.

No candle lit romantic evenings in our house!

We are newly married and have this adorable kitten who we consider our "child." On some evenings we like to light candles throughout the bedroom or living room to give it a romantic look. Well, every time we do this, our "child" goes about extinguishing each candle one at a time by placing her paw directly on the flame. After she does this, she has a look on her face... I swear she thinks she has just saved us from a terrible mishap. We have tried time again to show her as we light the candles that they are not a danger but she insists they be put out. We had one romantic evening last week when my husband suggested we leave Ginger outside and simply close the door. It worked!

How to beat a traffic ticket!

My dogs never saved my life, but they sure did save me from the law. I got pulled over to the side of the road by a police officer for speeding. I was guilty and was going to accept my punishment—a ticket that would cost about $150. I rolled down the window and when he approached my four dogs, three cats and a bird starting screaming, screeching and yelling so loud that it was embarrassing. I tried every way to shut them up but they simply wouldn't stop. The officer was so unnerved that he was afraid to reach in and take my license and registration. He simply said, "Lady, please drive slower and have a nice day." Thanks to my brood, the remainder of the day was great.

Oh, my god! I have lost my girlfriend's dog.... What am I going to do?

What a dilemma, this guy was fit to be tied and didn't know what to do. He was walking the dog when the leash broke and the dog took off down the street. He ran after him as the dog turned the corner. He started to laugh as he remembered the scene in the movie *Meet the Parents*, envisioning that he would have to find an exact duplicate of her dog or she would kill him. As he rounded the corner, there was Henry chatting with a lady friend and he picked him up and carried him back home.

Do You Treat Your Pet As If It Were Your Child?

Choose at first sight! When you first met your spouse to be, if he/she was allergic to your pet, what would you do?

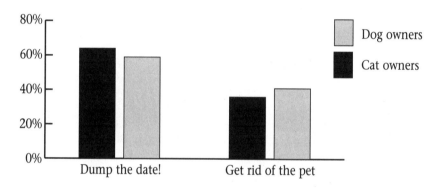

Barry says: Remember these are the real real pet lovers and so it shouldn't come as a surprise that if the new human in their life was allergic to the family pet, it would be bye bye to the date. Over 60 percent of our respondents said they would indeed dump the date.

On the other hand, nearly 40 percent said they would "get rid of the pet"... but alas, these people are nobody's fools. Most told us they would ship off their beloved pet to mom or dad or someone they know to watch over them until they were positive that this indeed would be a long time relationship. So they really wouldn't be getting rid of the pet.

Who are the traitors? It's those who are under 24 who are most likely to cast aside their pet in favor of love.

Pet napped? What to do!
How much ransom would
you pay to get your pet back?

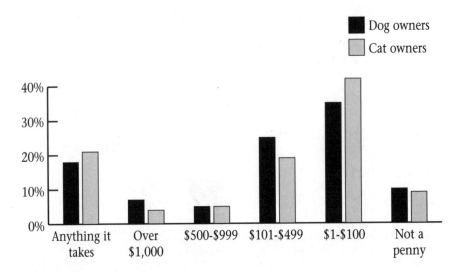

Barry says: 20 percent of our pet lovers would pay ANY-THING to get them back if they were pet napped. With cat lovers were a bit more willing to pay anything.

An absolutely heartless 10 percent told us they wouldn't pay anything to get a pet napped pet back. The heartless tight-wads are apt to be men 25 to 44 years old, who actually are in the biggest earning group, $75 k+ a year.

 For you statistical lovers, our average pet owner would be $823 in ransom to get their beloved pet back if pet napped.

Would you risk own life to save your pet? Have you ever? Has your pet ever saved someone's life?

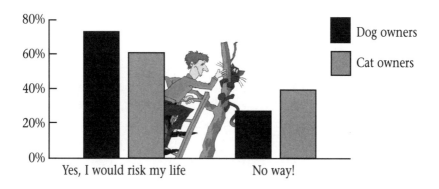

Barry says: What a wonderful group of pet lovers we have. Can you imagine that two-thirds of our respondents have said that "Yes, indeed, they would risk their own life to save their pet."

Marlo says: Luckily only a very small percentage of our group has actually faced this most awful test. 5 percent have faced this daunting task and every one of them pushed aside the fear for their own life to actually save their pet's life and in every instance they were successful.

On the pet side of things, 3 percent of our pets have actually been in a situation to save someone's life and they, too, succeeded in every instance.

What words does your pet know and respond to— other than its own name and that of family members?

Sweetheart	Get me beer	Stop!
Heel	Leash	Where's your mouse?
Mommy's baby	Ball	Give me your paw
Dinner	Want to eat?	Down
Let's go	Fetch	Food
Turkey	Kiss	Come to bed
Lie down	Up	Bye-bye
Oh shit!	Water	Come here
Out	Beg	No
Get out of here!	Go to mommy	Go to daddy
Kill the bug!	No, no	Go pee
Go outside	Come inside	Cookie
Ice cream	Don't bite	Bad
Go potty	Naughty	Kill!
Scram	Want to take a bath?	Yummy
Do you want to eat?	Give me the ball	Get off the couch
I love you	Wanna go out?	Wanna go for a ride?
It's okay	Get off the couch	Are you hungry?

Any of these sound familiar to you?

Oops!
If you accidentally lost your pet due to your own stupidity, would you admit to it?

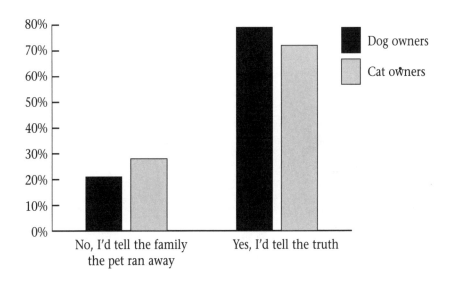

Marlo says: Some of us just can't own up to the truth. Nearly 25 percent of our pet owners told us that they would be afraid to tell the truth and instead tell the family that the pet simply ran away.

Once again these culprits are the men under 24 years old. Thankfully, three-quarters of us would fess up to the truth and immediately get a search party together.

Have you ever tried to lose your pet on purpose?

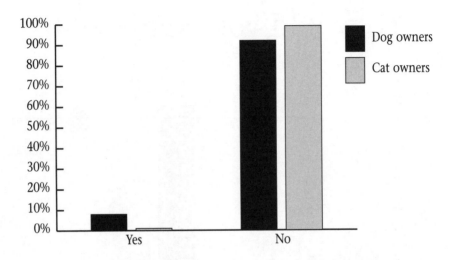

Barry says: My god, what is this country coming to? Eight percent of dog owners actually told us that have tried to lose their pet on purpose. Why in the world would they do that? By the way, it is most likely to be a woman aged 25-34 years old. On the other hand, kitties can relax. Only 1 percent of the cat owning population have admitted to this terrible deed.

As to actually going ahead and doing this deed, only 1 percent of the population admit to actually doing this and every one of them had regrets and nightmares and they deserve it.

Ok, so your pet is smarter than everyone else. What are your pet's best tricks?

Barry says: Some of the tricks listed below are not exactly those that it takes a whole lot to do, but take a look at the very special list of tricks at the bottom of the page.

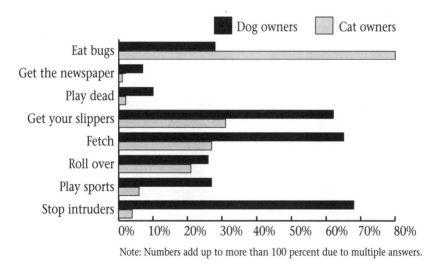

Note: Numbers add up to more than 100 percent due to multiple answers.

And the following is a sampling of those extra special tricks. Some of this is more than we need to know. Our canine and feline performers can also:

Open doors	Get beer from the fridge
Eat yarn (then choke)	Shake to and fro
Open beer cans	Bring rodents, etc. home
Pass gas on command	Sing
Hide and seek	Balance stuff on the nose

Scream at top of lungs when he/she sees us making love! Does your pet sleep in your room?

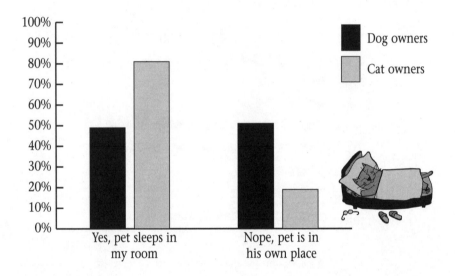

Marlo says: Who is sleeping with whom? We seem to prefer the company of our favorite feline over our cute canines. A lot more cats (81 percent) sleep with us than do dogs (49 percent).

We also asked the question of where they sleep if indeed they are in our room. 68 percent reported that our beloved pet sleeps in our bed. Those most likely to share the pillow and cover and sheets are single females from 18 to 34 years old, and young married couples under 24. The remainder of our pooches and kitties sleep on the floor or foot of the bed.

How much did you pay to acquire your pet?

For dog	Percent who spent this amount:	For cat
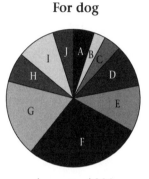	A Free B Under $10 C $10-$19 D $20-$49 E $50-$99 F $100-$199 G $200-$299 H $300-$399 I $400-$499 J $500 or more	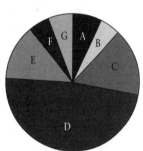
Average: $209		Average: $50

Marlo says: It makes perfect sense that acquiring a dog is significantly more expensive than a cat. Our dog lovers paid an average of $209 for their loving pet, while cat owners paid an average of $50.

We looked at those that were the big spenders and found that the 14 percent of dog owners who spent more than $400 were more likely to be in the 35-44 year old age group, with higher incomes and a few kids. We have a few individuals who spent over $2,000 for their dog, a few at $1,500. On the other end of the spectrum those who got their dog free of charge or paid less than $50 tended to be first time pet owners who are in the under 24 year old group.

Cat owners spend much less for their pet with the most expensive cat costing nearly $300. The few that spent that much were real cat lovers as they had an average of three cats and tended to be over 40 years old.

Ok, so is your pet worth what you paid for it?

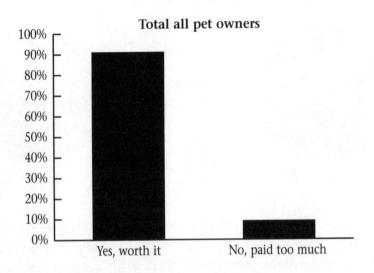

Barry says: Nearly all of our pet lovers, 91 percent, say that acquiring their pet was well worth it.

It is interesting to note that of the 9 percent who said that they "paid too much" for their pet, it is always the person in the family who DID NOT buy the pet. So if Dad bought it, it is Mom who said he spent too much money, and if it is Mom who bought it, it is Dad who says "she spent too much money."

Not a surprise, don't you agree?

Ok, pet lover. What other pets if any do you have besides your dog or cat?

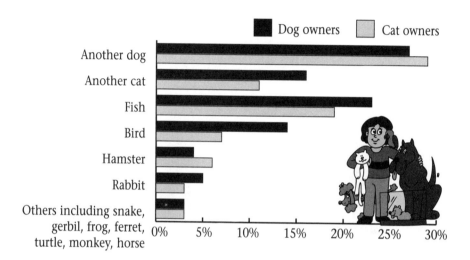

Americans have their own three-ring circus right in their own homes: We love pets, pets of all kinds. 61 percent of dog owning households have at least one other pet while 52 percent of cat owning households likewise have at least one other pet.

16 percent of households have at least two dogs.
29 percent of households have at least two cats.
35 percent of households have a dog and a cat.

On average both dog and cat owners have an average of nearly 1.7 other animals living in their household.

Does your pet get upset when you're roughhousing with a family member?

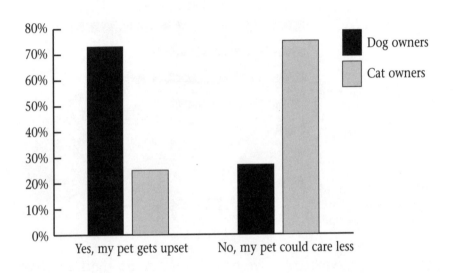

Yes, my pet gets upset   No, my pet could care less

- Dog owners
- Cat owners

Barry says: As you can see, our dogs are watching us all the time and 73 percent of them just don't like us to be roughhousing with anyone that is not them. That is with your child, spouse, neighbor, whomever. Cats, on the other hand, are really passive as only 25 percent even look in your direction.

If your pet does get upset, what if anything, does it do?

Answers among those who say their pets get upset at rough-housing!

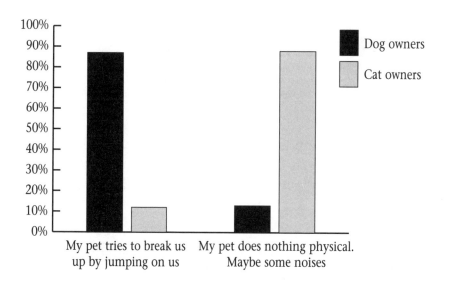

Barry says: It's a mirror image. The dogs (87 percent) try to join in and stop the roughhousing while the cats (88 percent) for the most part could care less about taking any action.

What type of food does your pet like best?

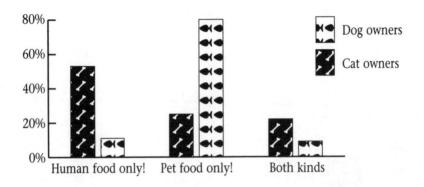

Cat food manufacturers are breathing a sigh of relief, because cats overwhelmingly DO NOT like human food. A mere pittance—20 percent—prefer it over our food. For a whopping 75 percent of the dogs, human food is the preference when given a choice. This would mean that dog food manufacturers had better start improving their products—adding more chicken, beef and other tasty treats.

What are the strangest things your pet eats?

CAUTION: Read this page before eating!

Strangest foods eaten by BOTH dogs and cats:

Burgers (cats like McDonalds while dogs like Burger King)
Spaghetti
Bubble gum
Onions
Ice Cream
Cheese curls

Dogs' strangest foods	Cats' strangest foods
Hide and seek	Balance stuff on the nose
Cooked peas and carrots	Raw potatoes
Watermelon	Pop tarts
Popcorn	Lizards
Diet Coke	Bugs, rodents, spiders
Fried egg	Olives
Donuts—chocolate only!	Pistachio nuts—shelled
Beer—preferably lite	Live fish from kid's tank
Pizza with extra cheese	Anything that lives outside
Toothpaste	Strawberry shortcake
Nachos	Chablis wine
Cream of wheat	Aluminum foil

Does your pet have bad breath? If yes, how do you take care of it?

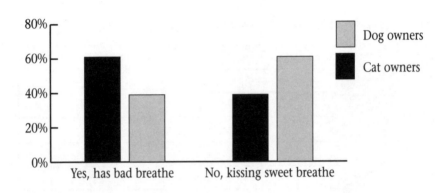

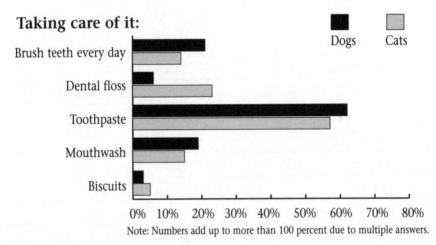

Note: Numbers add up to more than 100 percent due to multiple answers.

We smell (no pun intended) a great market for the manufacturers of pet products. Surprisingly, 65% of our pet owners DO NOTHING about bad breath. But those who care and do the above are quite ingenious and if some smart manufacturer comes out with a product, it seems it would be very successful.

Does your pet get along with other animals?

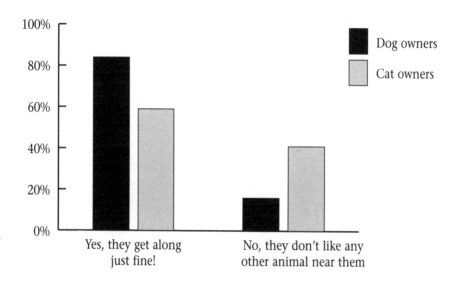

100% | 80% | 60% | 40% | 20% | 0%

■ Dog owners
▫ Cat owners

Yes, they get along just fine!

No, they don't like any other animal near them

Marlo says: Hey folks, we tell it like it is. Dogs are much more friendly than cats, but the majority of both get along just fine with other animals. Only 16 percent of our dog owners say that their pooch doesn't get along with other animals, while 41 percent of cat owners tell us that there is lots of hissing, scratching and general dislike for other animals on their turf.

Does you pet look like anyone you know? You? Your spouse? Your mother-in-law? Or who?

Marlo says: A very strange question gets a very strange answer. Doesn't one follow the other? Nearly half of all our pet owners and lovers (48 percent) tell us that, yes, their pooch or kitty bears an uncanny resemblance to their spouse! They are talking looks and or mannerisms etc. Much like our children pick up mannerisms that we have, it appears so do our pets.

Interestingly, 53 percent of the men and only 7 percent of the women say that their feline looks like their spouse. Thus putting the feline very much in the classic female column.

Most popular lookalikes other than spouse are, in order:

| Mother-in-law |
| An old teacher |
| The boss |
| Son-in-law |
| Daughter-in-law |
| Federal Express driver |
| Butcher |

Does your cat purr when it's picked up?

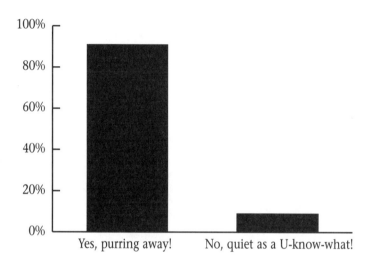

100% ┐

80%

60%

40%

20%

0%

Yes, purring away!   No, quiet as a U-know-what!

Marlo says: Purring is surely your cat's domain. It shows real, real love for their owners when they are picked up. Cats just love to purr to show their affection when they are picked up.

Does you pet tell you, "I hate pet food" and if so do you serve it anyway?

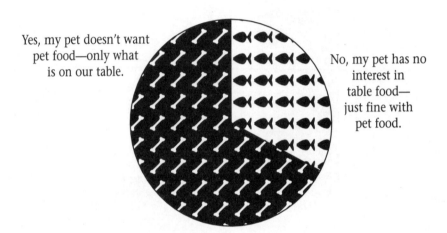

Yes, my pet doesn't want pet food—only what is on our table.

No, my pet has no interest in table food— just fine with pet food.

Marlo says: Two-thirds of our pets want to sit at the table and eat the delicious food that we eat.

So what do our pet lovers do? 76 percent of all owners tell us that they ignore what their pest want MOST of the time and feed them pet food. Many do admit to sneaking them a bite of leftovers here and there.

Do you remember your pet's birthday? If so, do you celebrate it?

Nope, don't remember it most of the time

I never forget my pet's birthday

Marlo says: Celebration! These answers take the cake (pun intended). Talk about loyalty and love for our pets. Take a look at these facts:

- 25 percent of all pet owners actually "celebrate"—be it a card, streamers, balloons, etc.

- 11 percent of all pet owners never forget to get a cake. That's right, they actually get a cake. It might be liver for the cat and a chicken cake for the dog, but they light the candles, sing happy birthday, and do all the things we do for our kids and for ourselves. Talk about dedication and real, real love.

- The group most responsible for parties and cakes and all the trimmings is all over the place, but you can be sure to find the women in the 35 to 44 year old category as the most likely to do it.

Do you ever call your spouse or child by your pet's name?

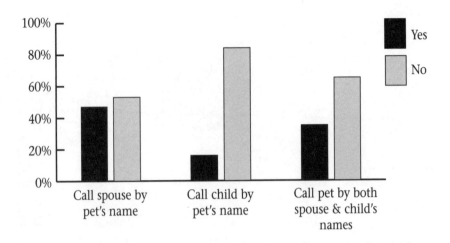

Marlo says: Confusion reigns everywhere and are you surprised?

47 percent of us call our spouse by the pet's name. We are a bit more cautious with the kids for some reason, as only 16 percent of us call our kids by the pet's name. 35 percent of us reverse course and call the pet by both our spouse's and child's name.

An additional tidbit: Women are more likely than men to:

Refer to their spouse by the dog's name
Call the dog by their spouse's name

In other words—men, you're often thought of as in the dog house! Maybe pay back for the mother-in-law jokes?

Ok, your pet talks to you! What does it say?

Marlo says: No doubt about it, animals are extremely talented according to our pet lovers. Talking dogs and cats can be found in nearly all of our homes. 84 percent report that pets indeed are like Dr. Doolittle as they talk to the humanils!

So what do these talented pets say?

Cats meowing to get our attention cry like a baby. Dogs are barking for attention as well as whining!

Here's a list of the other less common things that our animals are saying to us:

Come here
Play with me
More water, please!
Pet me, please!
Don't you touch her!
I love you
And the most common animalspeak.....hurry up, I have to go real bad!

Who's more kissable...
dogs or cats?

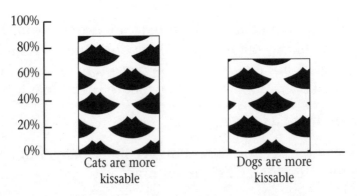

Marlo says: In case you are confused this is about us kissing them! Our cat lovers are much more affectionate (89 percent) than the dog lovers (71 percent) but in both cases we just love to kiss them and kiss them often. Where do we kiss them, say you?

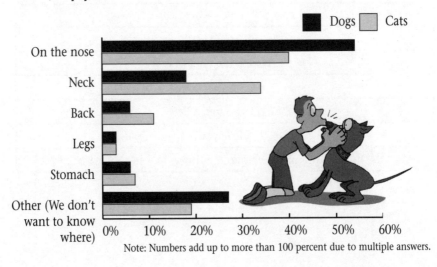

Note: Numbers add up to more than 100 percent due to multiple answers.

Do you let your pet lick your face?

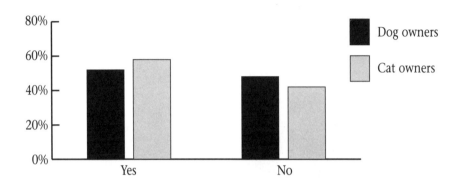

Marlo says: While 89 percent of us can't give our cat enough kisses, only 58 percent allow them the privilege to reciprocate. Is that fair to our cats? As to the pooch in our lives, 71 percent kiss them all the time, but again, only 52 percent are allowed to kiss us.

Can you imagine if these were the facts with our spouses? Big trouble for all would be the order of business.

The fussiest non-kissing, least affectionate group are the men who are over 40 (maybe they have had enough kisses in their lifetime, already from many different places).

Where does your pet sit in the car?

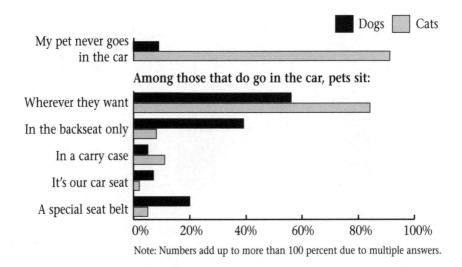

Dogs Cats

My pet never goes in the car

Among those that do go in the car, pets sit:

Wherever they want

In the backseat only

In a carry case

It's our car seat

A special seat belt

0%   20%   40%   60%   80%   100%

Note: Numbers add up to more than 100 percent due to multiple answers.

Marlo says: Another instance of the love we have for our pets is when we hit the road, at least for our dog. Nearly all (91 percent) love to take a ride with us. Cats seem to like staying at home as only 9 percent take to the road.

I find it interesting that some of our pets have their own car seat or even a seat belt. More love than you can imagine.

Here are some other startling facts: 11 percent of our pets have traveled with us on a plane and they are so special that virtually all of the cats are with us at the seat, while more than two thirds (68 percent) of the dogs are likewise at our sides. No compartments underneath the plane for our pets. We pay extra to have them right with us.

What are your pet's favorite foods that you eat as well?

Dogs' favorites	Cats' favorites
Pasta	Pasta
Lobster	Lobster
Clams	Clams
Steak	Meatballs
Ice cream	Spaghetti
Flounder	Trout
Roast turkey	Macaroni and cheese
Ham bones	Taco Bell
Matzoh ball soup	Domino's pizza

People crackers are loved by both dogs and cats. These are not to be confused with animal crackers!

Marlo says: Our pets eat as good or better than most families do. Can you believe matzoh ball soup, taco bell and lobster (many of us can't even afford lobster for ourselves).

Do you ever bring your pet along when you visit relatives...invited or not?

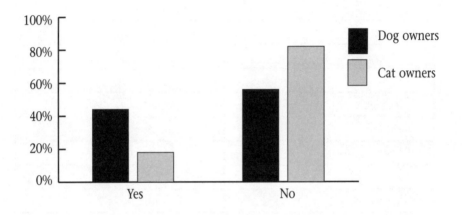

Marlo says: Ok, it may be controversial to say this as a bona fide animal lover. This is definitely one of my pet (pun intended) peeves. I think it is just not acceptable for someone to bring their pet into your home without being invited. I also think it is rude for them to even ask if they can bring them. That is my opinion! Do pet owners agree with me? Well 44 percent of dog owners bring them along when they go to visit relatives while only 18 percent bring their cats. So in the end it is a mixed bag when compared to my own opinion.

When asked about bringing them when they are NOT invited, we find that 40 percent of dog owners and only 21 percent of cat owners have told us that yes, they sometimes bring the pet along without asking permission. What do you think? Talk among yourselves.

Do you do it when your pet is in the room?

Ok, so I had to get at least one sex question in this book to spice it up.

- 77 percent of us said "sure, who cares, who looks, no problem."

- 23 percent of us said "gross, no way, I couldn't with him/her right in the bed with us.

- So we have a whopping 77 percent claiming they don't mind having a feline or canine voyeur in the same room as them.

Now if we could only get them to actually speak, that would be some book.

What is the most unusual way you indulge your pet?

Pet owners of America are like no other people in this world!

We indulge our pets in ways that we wouldn't even consider for ourselves or our spouses....or the kids. Pets are really very special, and wouldn't it be wonderful if we could hear what they are thinking as all of this attention comes their way.

The following are some of the very special privileges our canines and felines enjoy:

A daily massage!
Has her own swimming pool!
Gets a Snickers bar after dinner every night.
Eats ice cream with the family
Sleeps in our bed right on our pillows
Takes a bath or shower with me.
Doesn't like cold food, so it always goes into the microwave before he has to eat it.
Drinks from his own glass....no bowls for him.
Has her own bed, complete with an electric blanket
Has pajamas that match his dad (my husband)
Has a different outfit to wear every day. One for each day of the week.
Has a special little door so that she can go outside whenever she wants ...do her business or lounge around and come back in.

When you come home, who do you greet first?

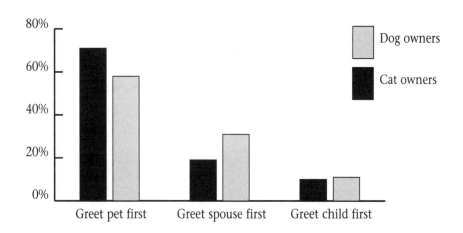

Dog owners

Cat owners

Barry says: This is one of those questions that I like so much, because it is one that we probably never think about—it just happens. Approximately 65 percent of us are first greeted by our beloved pet before a single word is uttered to anyone else. Not a word, not a kiss, not a hello. The reason is clear. We give so much love to our pet, that he/she is always the first at the door to welcome us home. Our spouse is in the kitchen or watching tv or doing some such chore...the kids are doing homework, watching tv or simply sitting around the house. But no matter what they are doing, our pet will stop and rush to greet us.

Our wonderful spouses are next in line as they quickly make it to the door, 25 percent of them that is, to say "Hi, honey, how was your day?"

The children are last in line, probably intentionally because they are always too busy doing something. So when we tell you that 10 percent are at the door first, I am sure it is not a surprise.

If you are married and want to be first on the list, you are most likely over 40 years old and attentive enough to be at the door when your spouse arrives home.

Do you have a nickname for your pet?

Just as we discovered that a great majority of us have nick-names for each other, we found that nearly half (47 percent) of our pet owners do in fact have a special nickname other than the given name that they call to their pet. Some of them are strange, some are funny, some are unknown, and some are well you be the judge. Here is a list of some of the nicknames that we received from you:

Dogs' nicknames	Cats' nicknames
Pumpkin	Superman
Batman	The Beast
Luscious	Fur Face
Honey	Loaf
Dopey	Mothball
Angel Face	Coco and Chanel
Aladdin	Guido
Bones	Big Pussy
Fire and Ice	Purr Monster
Smith & Wesson	Wild One
Lucy	Ethel

Who did you meet first— your spouse or your pet?

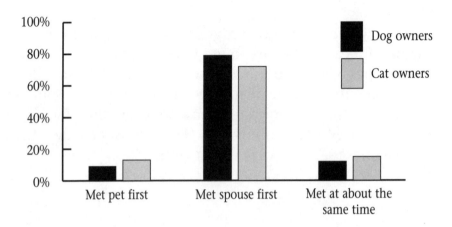

75 percent of us had met our real love, our spouse, before we met our pet. Approximately 11 percent of us were in love with our pet before we met our spouse and the remaining 14 percent said they met both at around the same time.

Marlo says: It looks like some of us took advantage of having a wonderful pet to find our spouse. It is not uncommon to see single people walking or playing with their pet, many hoping to meet someone of the opposite sex who either likes your pet, has their own pet, or uses the pet as an excuse to meet you.

Does your pet ever leap up into your arms?

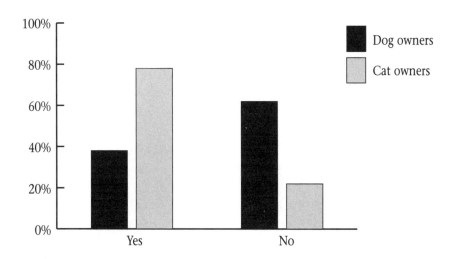

Marlo says: Leapin' lizards, jumping cats are more common (78 percent) then leapin' dogs (38 percent). It is usually by surprise and the percentage is low for dogs because remember the average dog weighs 44 pounds, quite a surprise if they could and would leap into your arms. Dogs get just as much lovin', but most of it is at ground level!

Death! Had/would have funeral? Details

Barry says: Not a pleasant subject, but we all have to face it at some time in our lives and that of our pets. 52 percent of pet owners say that indeed they would make a funeral for their pet, including a proper burial.

Look at these statistics:

- 62 percent of those who have had a pet pass away have indeed had a funeral for their pet.

- 21 percent of these people have told us that they bought and placed a headstone on the grave of their pet.

So it appears that much like in real life with our beloved ones, our pets are treated with the same dignity.

Women, Women, Women, Women Men, Men

This is our jeopardy question..errr answer. Above are the answers to the following six questions.

Who is in charge of:

- Buying food?

- Arranging for veterinarian visits?

- Bathing the pet?

- Grooming the pet?

- Walking the dog in the morning?

- Walking the dog in the evening?

Barry says: Men have the tougher job, they have to do their chores like the mailman. Walking the dog when it is freezing, sleeting, snowing, raining, light and dark and whether we are tired or not!

Does you dog pee upon meeting strangers?

Barry says: How did I get to comment on this question and why did we even ask it. Well, it's come to our attention that a great many female dogs act in this way when they meet the human male.

Do you really think this is true and limited to female dogs and human males and not male dogs and human females?

So that you won't be worried about this all day, only 11 percent of dogs are reported to do this deed. So if you are a strange man, keep your distance of the big, big dogs and make sure you are properly introduced.

Do you consider your pet friendly? That is, when they meet another pet?

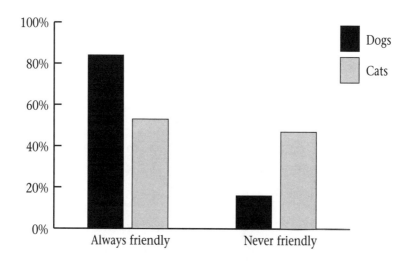

Marlo says: While the majority of our pets, 84 percent of dogs and 53 percent of cats, are always friendly towards other pets, it does concern us that 47 percent of cats are never ever friendly. No middle ground. They love you or hate you.

Dogs seem to be quite friendly when they meet another dog, especially one of the opposite sex. Not so for cats, they don't seem to care about gender.

Ok, tell the truth. Do you intentionally leave the radio/tv on for your pet's entertainment when you are out of the house?

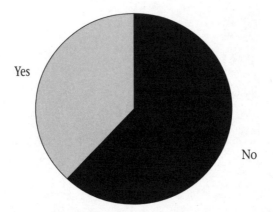

Yes

No

Barry says: With more than a third (38 percent) of our pet owners telling us that they always leave the radio/tv on, the question begs, does the pet ever change the channel? No, not yet. So if the owner likes CNN or MTV or soaps or talk shows, the pet is stuck with it.

Does your pet watch tv?

Barry says: Now that we have 500+ channels across the U.S., it is so hard to choose what to watch. While we make the choices, our pet owners have actually told us which shows their pet likes. This is not the Neilsen rating system for non-humans, but it is fascinating that 35 percent of dog owners and 31 percent of cat owners have told us they are convinced their pet actually sits and watches certain shows regularly. How do they know this?

They tell us that for most television programs and most pets, there is an obvious NO interest, while for others they sit and watch intently. This is not a measure of I.Q. either. But in the interest of those who may want to have their pet sit by their side to share some popcorn and beer and watch tv, here goes: (We are slightly ashamed to say we have listed them in rank order of their favorites.)

Dogs' favorite TV shows	Cats' favorite TV shows
1. *Oprah*	1. *Oprah*
2. *Rosie O'Donnell*	2. *Rosie O'Donnell*
3. *Who Wants to Be A Millionaire?*	3. *Who Wants to Be A Millionaire?*
4. *E.R.*	4. *Sex in the City*
5. *West Wing*	5. *Malcom in the Middle*
6. *Saturday Night Live*	6. Nickelodeon
7. *The Sopranos*	7. *Jerry Springer*
8. *Jerry Springer*	8. *Bugs Bunny*
9. Any cartoons	9. *Today Show*
10. *Today Show*	10. Cat food commercials

Note: This is not scientific. But Oprah, Rosie, and Regis sure know how to keep an audience. *Sex in the City*—it sort of makes sense for cats....many more female owners? *Sopranos*—same could be said....more male owners.

Does your pet wear clothing?

Americans have the best dressed pets in the entire world! Here is a look at the fashion plate pets of the United States of America. The latest in fashion includes:

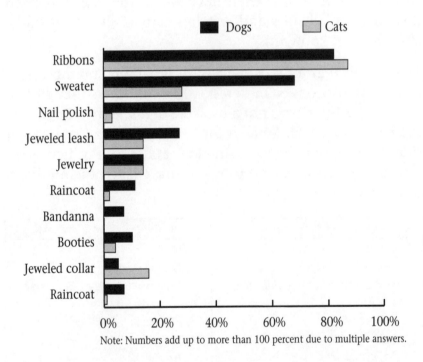

Note: Numbers add up to more than 100 percent due to multiple answers.

In the over the edge category of dress, believe this or not!

4 percent of our dog owners tell us that they dye their pet's hair frequently—most likely to match their own hair color or their favorite doggie outfits. The most creative people who are likely to actually do this are in the 18 to 24 year old group and, of course, they are all women.

In the unlikely event that both you and your pet required non-emergency treatment, who would you take care of first?

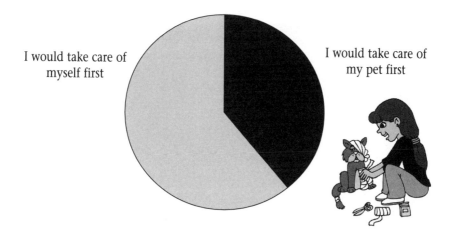

I would take care of
myself first

I would take care of
my pet first

Pets are people, too! Our respondents overwhelmingly said they would care for their pet before they would care for themselves. They, of course, feel that their pet would be helpless in this situation and so they need to be attended to first.

While helping the pet first was across the board, it was most likely to be the women ages 18 to 24 who would be unanimous. On the other hand, men in the 35 and over category would leave the treatment to their spouse and take care of themselves first.

How often do you take your pet to the vet?

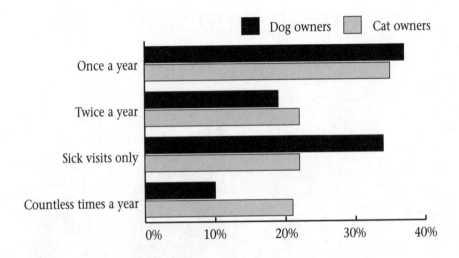

Barry says: Animal lovers take very good care of their pets, even more so than they do for themselves. A check of the above figures against what we do as a family indicates that pets' health is taken care of on a much better schedule than we do for ourselves. They are right there to get shots, check-ups and whatever is necessary to keep them content.

Grooming!
Do you have it done professionally and if so how much do you pay?

Barry says: When it comes to professional grooming, it's the dogs hands down who are treated royally. Dogs on average are groomed more often at a higher cost than most of their owners.

59 percent of dogs are professionally groomed, with 20 percent of them having a monthly appointment at a cost of $34.23. It should be noted that 5 percent of these lucky dogs (pun intended) are groomed at a cost of more than $60.56 on average! 62 percent of our dogs are groomed an average of 4.6 times a year.

Cats are left to themselves for the most part when it comes to professional grooming. Only 6 percent of cat owners bring kitty to be groomed and for the most part it happens 2 to 3 times a year. Grooming a cat costs on average $16.45.

How often do you bathe your pet at home?

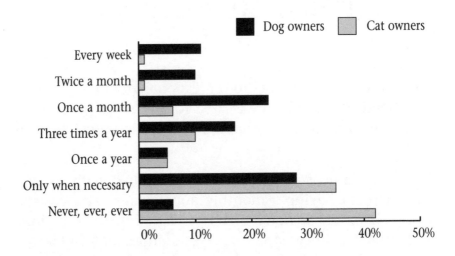

Marlo says: How would you like to be among the 30 some odd percent of pets that are bathed only when necessary or the 42 percent of cats that are never ever bathed? I think I would prefer to among the bulk of the dogs that are bathed at least once a month!

For those interested, dogs for the most part love to be bathed while, not surprisingly, cats are not fond of bath water.

If you got a divorce, who do you think would get custody of your pet?

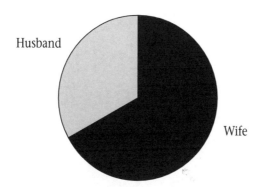

Husband

Wife

Barry says: If you are headed for a divorce and you're male, you can be virtually sure that you won't stand a chance against your wife—even if it was or is known to be "your pet." So be prepared to say goodbye to the wife, the house and now even the pet!

As far as we can tell the only males that have a chance to get the pet in a custody battle are those over 45 who have a healthy income and really put up a fight. The rest of you can forget it!

Ok, so this next question is obvious to follow the previous question:

IF YOU ARE DIVORCED, was your pet a custody issue during the proceedings? And were visiting privileges granted to the loser?

No, it was not an issue and did not come up

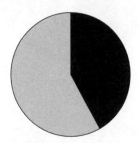

Yes, it was an issue in the divorce proceedings

Barry says: Pets indeed were a point of controversy in 42 percent of divorce proceedings. This is up from just a few years ago when it was 31 percent. Neither party wanted to give up their four-legged buddy.

As previously noted, the woman prevailed most often and it was even more one sided than when we asked what if you were to get a divorce as 89 percent of the women won versus the perceived number of 67 percent.

As to visiting privileges, forget about it. Men won the privilege in only 3 percent of the cases with the other 97 percent being told, say goodbye, no visits!

Do you ever give cards and presents that come from your PET to YOUR FAMILY?

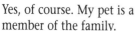

Yes, of course. My pet is a member of the family.

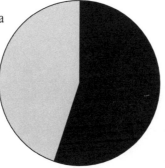

Are you kidding?
Cards/presents from
my pet to my family!

Barry says: A bulletin for the greeting card companies! There are cards for just about every occasion and every situation you can think of, and pet owners love to send cards from the family pet to dad, mom, and grandma and grandpa. 56 percent of our pet owning families actually include a greeting card from their pet for a birthday, anniversary, Christmas, etc. As to gifts, 38 percent take it a step further and buy a present for mom, dad, sis and say it is from the pet.

Do you ever exercise with your pet?
If "yes," what do you do?

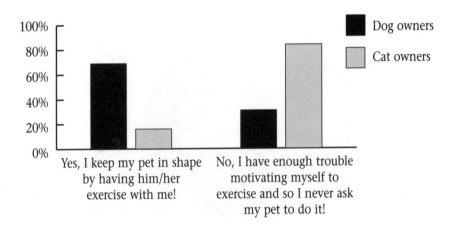

Barry says: Do we love our dogs or what? Some 69 percent of us exercise regularly with our pooch—although 79 percent are claiming that the old "walking the dog" routine constitutes a form of exercise. Personally, we prefer the more creative types as the "real deal:" 12 percent take the dog hiking, 8 percent camping, 19 percent take their dog for a swim regularly and of course in this age of running 39 percent have their dog alongside them as they do their morning or evening jog.

As for cats, I find it impossible to even fathom that 16 percent say that they have their cat exercise with them. But a look at the statistics finds that 95 percent consider walking the cat as exercise and I don't really consider that as a bona fide exercise. The remaining 5 percent say they have the cat running with them and quite frankly I find that a stretch.

Can your pet open doors?

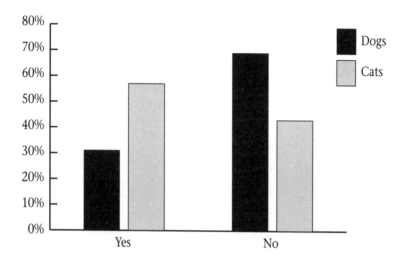

Barry says: Cats win this contest paws down! More cats (57 percent) than dogs (31 percent) can push open those doors.

Do you carry PICTURES in your wallet?
If yes, tell us how many and who are they?

Barry says: Ok, we tried a stupid human trick question. We simply asked a general question to all our pet owners: Do you carry pictures in your wallet and, if yes, how many and who are they?

Of course by this time most of our respondents knew what we were really getting at: Are pictures of the poodle and snapshots of the siamese in there?

Well, first things first: 91 percent of us do carry pictures with us.

82 percent of us carry photos of the kids, 61 percent carry photos of the spouse, and 44 percent of the family pet. Only 2 percent carry pictures of their mother-in-law...meaning that 20 times as many people carry pictures of their pet than their mothers-in-law.

As to the numbers game, we carry a total of 8 pictures, 4 to 6 of the kids, 2 to 4 of the spouse and 1 to 2 of our pet.

Is your pet named in your will? If so, what will it inherit?

Barry says: Nearly 30 percent of our pets don't know how lucky they are because they have actually been named in their owner's will.

Not surprisingly, it's the older 45+ set—those who are perhaps more prone to thinking about their own mortality—who have done this great deed. Generally it is the older single or married without children who have done this, although we do have many families who have at least set aside something for their pet.

Some have told us that they have left enough so that their pet will be able to be cared for in the style they are accustomed to for the rest of their lives. In terms of actual money left for whatever, the range is from $100 to $10,000 a year for these pets who will hit the lottery if their owner passes on.

When you take home a doggie bag, what do you really do with it?

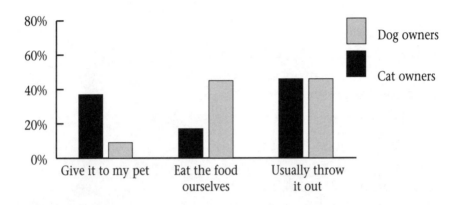

Barry says: At least one-third of the dog owners really do give the "doggie bag" to their dog. The largest percentage (46) however, do what I do. We take it home, hold it for a few days, forget that we have it and finally throw it out. 17 percent did tell us that they, in fact, eat the leftovers, which is a good idea and we sometimes do that as well.

Cats once again get the short end of the "doggie bag" or should it be called a "cat bag" in this case. Only 9 percent of our cat owners told us that they give their little leftovers to the cat to eat the next day. However, nearly half (45 percent) of our owners can't wait to eat it themselves. Why do you think that cat owners are nearly three times more likely to actually eat the "doggie bag" contents than are dog owners? And finally, as with the dog owners, 46 percent simply hold it for a few days, forget they have it or simply decide to throw it out.

Hey, when do we get to eat?

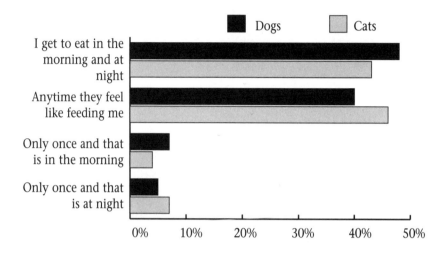

Barry says: It appears that approximately 6 percent of our pet lovers, don't love them enough to feed them until the evening meal, which by the way is their only meal. I think it is a bit cruel to make our little friends wait so long to eat and then make it the only meal of the day. Other than the end of the day, about 5 percent of our canine and feline friends only have to wake up and then they get their one and only meal of the day.

Nearly half of us are quite more regimented as they feed their pets both in the morning and again at night. Another large percentage of us allow our little friends to eat several times throughout the day. As best as we can tell, those that eat at many times during the day are the most content.

Do you try to spend a specific amount a week for pet food? And, aside from food, how much do you spend on your pet a year?

With the cost of living today, can you blame anyone? Approximately 10 percent of our pet owners actually set aside a budget for pet food. The most budget conscious people are likely to be in the 18 to 34 year old age group and be single women.

What's the budget, you ask? $13.45 feeds the dog while $9.65 feeds the cat per week.

Let it never be said that we do not pamper our favorite felines and canines. About 8 percent of both dogs and cats have owners who spend more than $1,200 a year to please them. The money covers everything you can imagine and some you can't... jewelry? Hope my wife doesn't see this.

As for the remaining 92 percent of pet owning population: on average, we spend $204.65 for our dog and $154.23 for our cat each year. This, of course, includes visits to the vet, toys, clothing and other assorted essentials.

Feeding your pet...from the table, on the table, lick the plate, share the food directly with your pet?

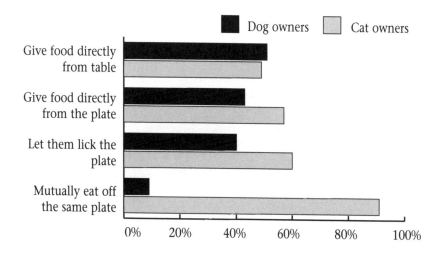

Dog owners ■   Cat owners ▨

Give food directly from table

Give food directly from the plate

Let them lick the plate

Mutually eat off the same plate

0%   20%   40%   60%   80%   100%

Barry says: It looks like about half of us like to share and get intimate with our pets, but I am glad to see that we draw the line at mutually eating from the same plate.

Is your pet named after someone?

Much like the names that we select for our children, many times the name means "something special" to us. In fact 28 percent of all pet owners told us that yes, they did indeed name their pet for "someone".

That "someone" includes:

Family members
Mother-in-law
Sports heroes
Old girl/boy friends
TV celebrities
Themselves
Things they can't afford (e.g. cars, designer clothing, etc.)
Bosses that they love or hate
People they think look like their pet

Which of the following fictional characters best embodies your pet's personality?

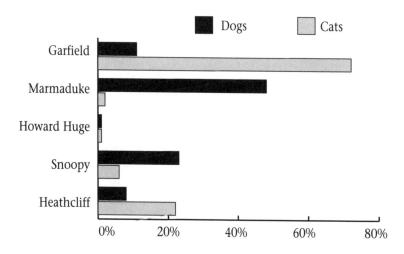

A pet can sure have a weird personality! Approximately 72 percent of cat owners feel that their cat's personality is a lot like Garfield's, but 6 percent said the personality fits Snoopy who is, as you know, a dog. While dog owners overwhelmingly selected Marmaduke (48 percent) and Snoopy (23 percent) as the closest personalities, 11 percent thought of Garfield who, of course, is a cat.

In other words, some members of this group probably have cats that chew bones and dogs that eat lasagna.

When you spouse is away, does your pet take their place on your spouse's side of the bed?

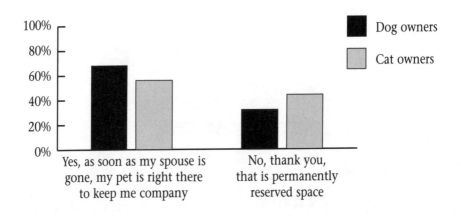

Barry says: "A warm body is a body"—so say our dog owners who are quick to tell us that 68 percent of them have their pooch sleeping right by their side when the spouse is away.

A bit more than half of us (56 percent) feel the same about their cat taking the place of the spouse when they are away.

Interestingly enough, it is the women 18 to 24 who feel most protected by their dog when their husband is away. As to our cats, it is just about all the women who don't mind having their feline in bed with them when hubby is gone. Men, on the other hand, could care less about having a canine or feline in the bed, most likely those who are over 40.

Is your pet allowed free access to all rooms in the house?

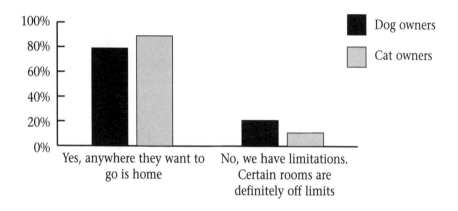

Marlo says: Sure our pets are members of the family and so it figures that over 85 percent have a free pass to roam the home.

The remaining 15 percent are limited and most of it seems reasonable. They have told us that they don't want them on the sofa, in the kitchen and certainly not in the bedroom on their bed.

What is your pet's favorite toy?

Far be it from us to destroy widely-held beliefs, but not all cats prefer spools of yarn. Sure, there are some that love that yarn—in fact it is 21 percent. But cats have a wide range of preferential toys, such as plastic bones, socks (men's socks are preferred), balls of all kinds, string and, of course, catnip (that's a toy?). There are also the more "upscale" kitties out there who, when it comes to leisure time, prefer squeaky toys, stuffed animals, rawhide bones, and dolls?

Dogs tell us that their favorites include socks (men's), string, stuffed animals, dolls, and of course, the usual balls and rawhide bones.

How did you come to choose your actual pet?

Animals out there, listen up! Here's how you can be sure to get adopted quickly if you're currently a single and unattached animal.

About 37 percent of people surveyed will adopt you if you're looking particularly cute. Can you look cute, smile, jump up and lick continuously? If you're the most boisterous one in the bunch, 27 percent of prospective owners are most likely to choose you as a new member of the family. So ask your fellow single pets what boisterous means and do it! Conversely, 20 percent of pet owners might decide you're tops if you're the runt of the litter. So if you are a small guy or gal, make your way up front and just look droopy-eyed—that says "please pick me, I am so little, I need a home."

We feel sorry for the 18 percent of pets who weren't chosen for their charming personality of great looks. I hope they can't read this or that their owner will not read it to them, but they were selected because (drum roll please) they were *the only ones left.*

Of course, it's better to be adopted no matter what the reason, as opposed to not be taken at all.

Games people play...How about games that pets play!

No bones (no pun) about it, all pets like to play. While dogs are more athletic, cats are into physical fitness as well.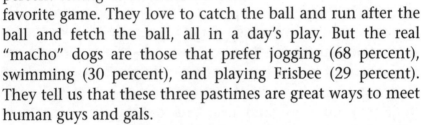

Dogs are the ball players, with 87 percent telling us that that is their favorite game. They love to catch the ball and run after the ball and fetch the ball, all in a day's play. But the real "macho" dogs are those that prefer jogging (68 percent), swimming (30 percent), and playing Frisbee (29 percent). They tell us that these three pastimes are great ways to meet human guys and gals.

As for cats, there aren't any wussies out there. Nearly 40 percent of cats jog daily, 8 percent actually swim, and 5 percent can actually catch or fetch a Frisbee. Playing with some type of ball—be it yarn or whatever—especially catch, ranks as the all-time favorite of cats at 91 percent.

Does your pet get along with strangers?

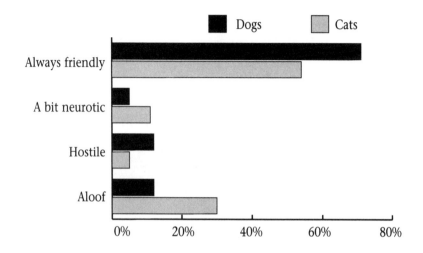

Barry says: Dogs display a friendlier disposition than cats (71 percent to 54 percent). Nonetheless, mail carriers everywhere should still be on the lookout, because some of our pets are  a bit testy, hostile if you will— a few are surely neurotic.

The neurotic animals need to see a "shrink" and we cover that issue within the next few pages.

Does your pet get upset when you're making love to someone?

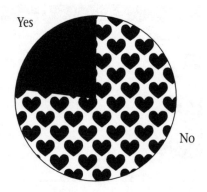

Yes

No

Barry says: As one who has written many books about love and sex, I of course had to ask this question and the answers were interesting.

The results again show that both cats and dogs are avid voyeurs: 77 percent indicate that their pets don't mind sitting back, chewing on something and just observing. Must be vicarious thrills for our canines and kitties.

Yet while many couples told us that their cats seem to be mesmerized by their lovemaking, dogs, on the other hand, are not quite that passive. We've been told by quite a few that their dog will sometimes attack them at a very inappropriate time during their lovemaking session. All in good playful fun (we hope).

Do you think your pet needs a shrink? If so, have you ever actually done it? Did it help?

We've previously established that we indeed have hostile and neurotic pet—dogs that act like cats, cats that act like dogs, cats that sleep with dolls, and dogs that watch Oprah. So is it any wonder that 18 percent claim that, yes, their pet indeed needs a shrink?

But, as in all things, money factors into the equation, and less than 8 percent of pet owners have actually taken their pet to a shrink. (Interestingly enough, nearly all of these particular owners reported that they themselves visit a psychiatrist on a regular basis.)

Of those who have actually taken their pets to an animal shrink, 62 percent report that their pet has benefited from the therapy. Alas, most wouldn't let us in on what was discussed during the sessions. They sighted animal-owner-doctor confidentiality.

Does your partner have a problem with your pet sleeping in your bed?

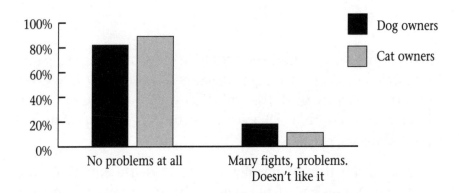

Hey, only 18 percent of dog owners and 11 percent of cat owners have jealous partners who object to letting sleeping dogs lie...in the bed, that is. We thought it would be a much higher number!

Would leave home without it?

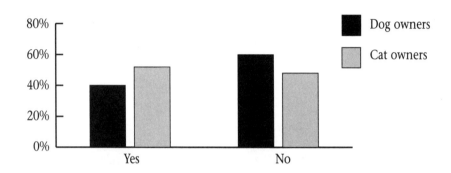

We're talking about your pet, not your credit card! Nearly half of owners would rather not go on vacation if the only option they had was to place their beloved pet in a kennel. Amazing!

These extremely caring owners are most likely to be single women. The dog owners are likely to be 25 to 34 years old, while the cat owners are the younger females 18 to 24 years old.

Who do you love bestest?

Barry says: I sometimes ask my grandchildren, who do they like best including everyone in their life we could think of, other grandparents, mom, dad, pets, friends by name, etc. So in this question we asked our pet owners to tell us in rank order who they love best. So, guess who's number 1! That's right, your spouse (thank god what a relief!). The love scale continues as follows:

Spouse (whew!)
Children
Mom and Dad
Pet
Siblings
Bosses
And in last place: Mothers- and fathers-in-law

We think it is only fair to report that 3 percent of our respondents did put their love for their pets in the #1 spot, ahead of everyone else in their world.

And it should be noted that siblings, bosses and in-laws are ranked below our beloved pets.

Tell us what you named your pet

Dogs' names	Cats' names
Bootsie	Coco
Quinc	MacHeath
Roxy	Black Magic
Bum	Claw-deus
Sherlock	Chastity
Animal	Whimper
Toto	Patches
Furston	Columbine
Ms. Roosevelt Mac	Boo kitty
PB Max	Alda
Brittney	Justin
Hershey	D.C.
Buckwheat	Macbeth
Taffy	Boarder
Ringo	Fuzz
Peanut	Tasha
Kudo	Velcro
Spirit	Slim Cat
Polo	Rocky
Jupiter	Fat Boy
Quincy	Hawkeye
Jennifer	Brad
Ricky	Lucy

What are the main reasons you have a pet?

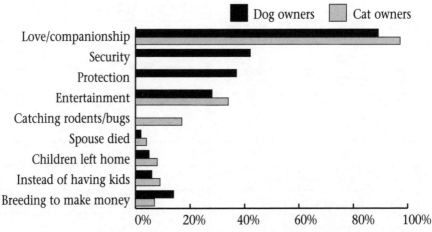

Note: Numbers add up to more than 100 percent due to multiple answers.

Love and companionship, of course, say 93 percent of the pet-owning population. But note the other reasons for having a pet are different when it comes to a dog or a cat. Americans feel that dogs provide security, protection and entertainment. While cats too, provide entertainment, they are also owned because they are stars when it comes to catching those pesky rodents or bugs.

Who are these people?
Demographics

The following are some interesting statistics about the people (and the pets) who responded to our survey:

- A total of 5,345 people answered our questionnaires. The respondents came from all 50 states, urban, suburban and rural areas.

- We had 62 percent female and 38 percent male respondents

- 74 percent of respondents are married, 11 percent are divorced/separated, 6 percent are single, 4 percent are widow/widowers and the remainder are in a variety of situations including engaged, living with someone, etc.

- The average age of our respondents was 38 years old.

- The average income of our respondents is $43,321 a year.

- 57 percent of the respondents had some form of college education.

- 59 percent have children at home.

- 93 percent live in a private home.

- 39 percent live in the suburbs.

- 24 percent live in urban areas.

- The average respondent has 1.73 dogs and 1.95 cats.

- 65 percent have one dog.

- 59 percent have one cat.

- The average number of years the pet has been a part of the family is 5.7 years.